The Birth of a Whale

By John Archambault
Illustrated by Janet Skiles

Silver Press
Parsippany, New Jersey

A humpback whale
sings its song, diving deep
through the deep water dark.

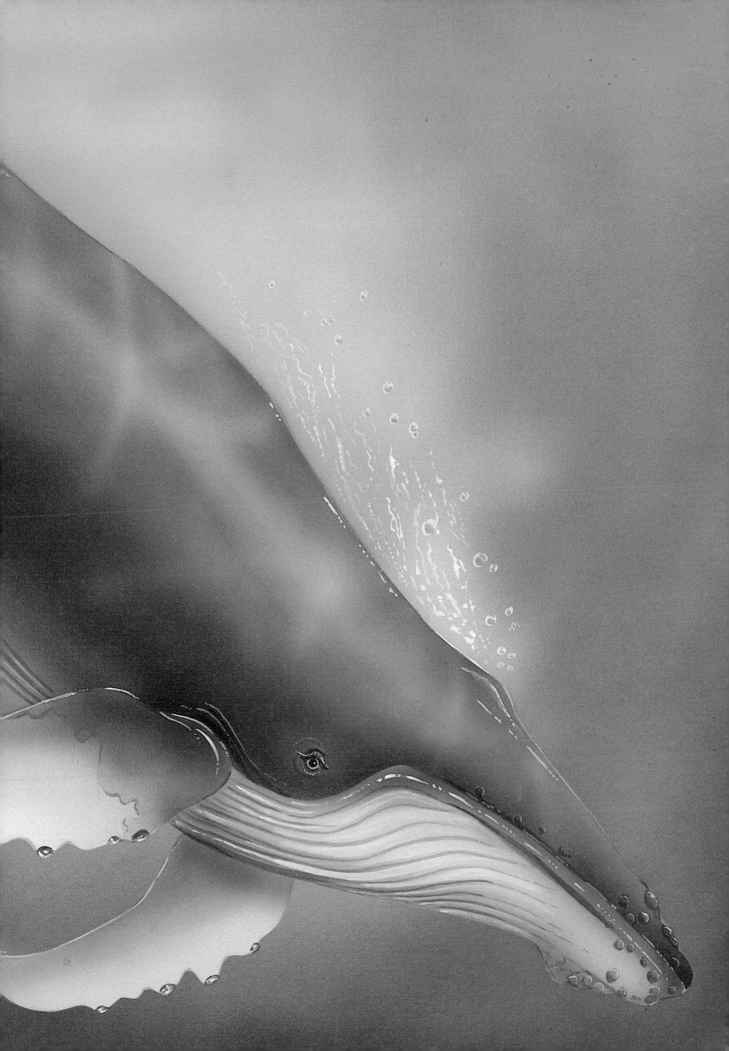

The deep water dark,
the deep water dark,
singing, dancing
in the deep water dark.

Singing songs and sounds to the ocean around, gently moving through the twilight sea, it comes…

A gentle giant
of power and might,
rolling forward,
rocking slowly,
a 50-ton mountain
of shadowy grace,
singing, dancing
in the deep water dark.

The deep water dark,
the deep water dark,
singing, dancing
in the deep water dark.

Humpback whales, males and females in joyous play, caress each other with their wing-like flippers...

Rubbing and touching,
lolling and rolling,
rising and diving, together,
in the deep water dark.

The deep water dark,
the deep water dark,
singing, dancing
in the deep water dark.

When a mother is ready
to birth her baby,
the male…nearby…
starts singing a song
to comfort and calm her.

The mother surfaces,
her white belly skyward,
waving her flippers
in the open air,
slapping her tail
on the moonlit water.

A breathless moment,
a family in concert,
a baby whale is being born,
in the deep water dark.

The deep water dark,
the deep water dark,
singing, dancing
in the deep water dark.

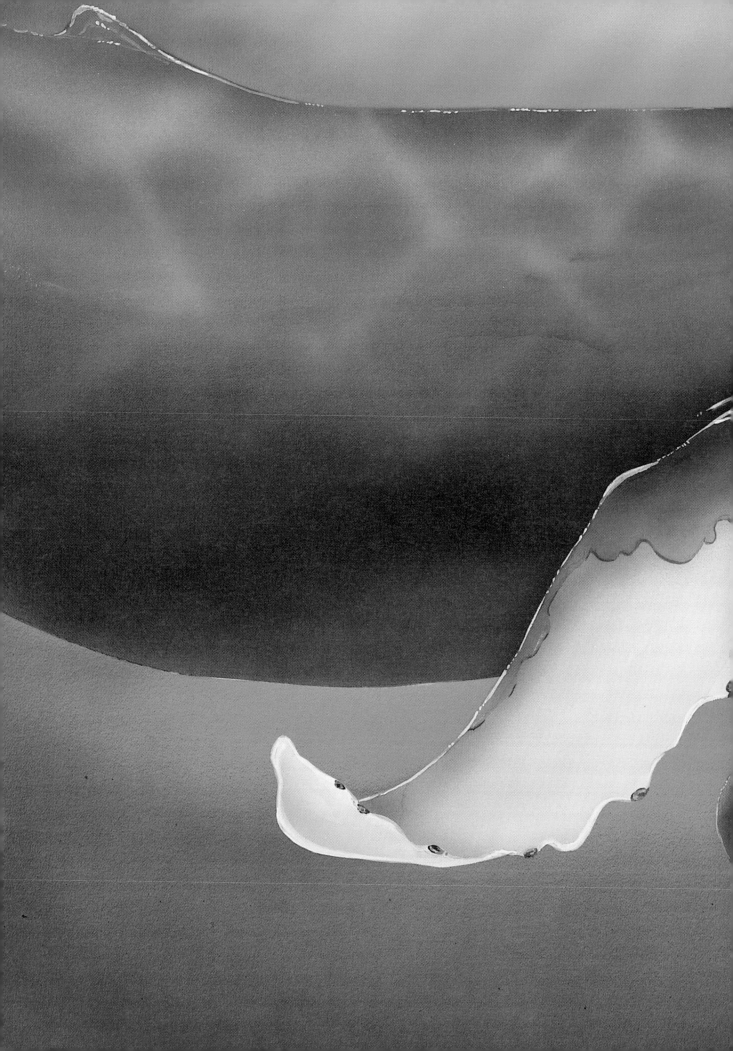

The baby whale is born
underwater, 15 feet long,
weighing three tons,
with blue eyes open...

But in danger of drowning.
In the first few seconds,
it must have air!

Nudged by its mother with no time to lose, rising frantically…frantically upward, the baby calf bursts above water searching for air. Puff! A full breat in the deep water dark.

The deep water dark,
the deep water dark,
singing, dancing
in the deep water dark.

The newborn whale has had its first lesson, learning to breathe… learning to live in both water and air.

A baby calf follows its mother,
a small blue shadow at her side,
breathing when she breathes,
diving when she dives.
In constant contact.

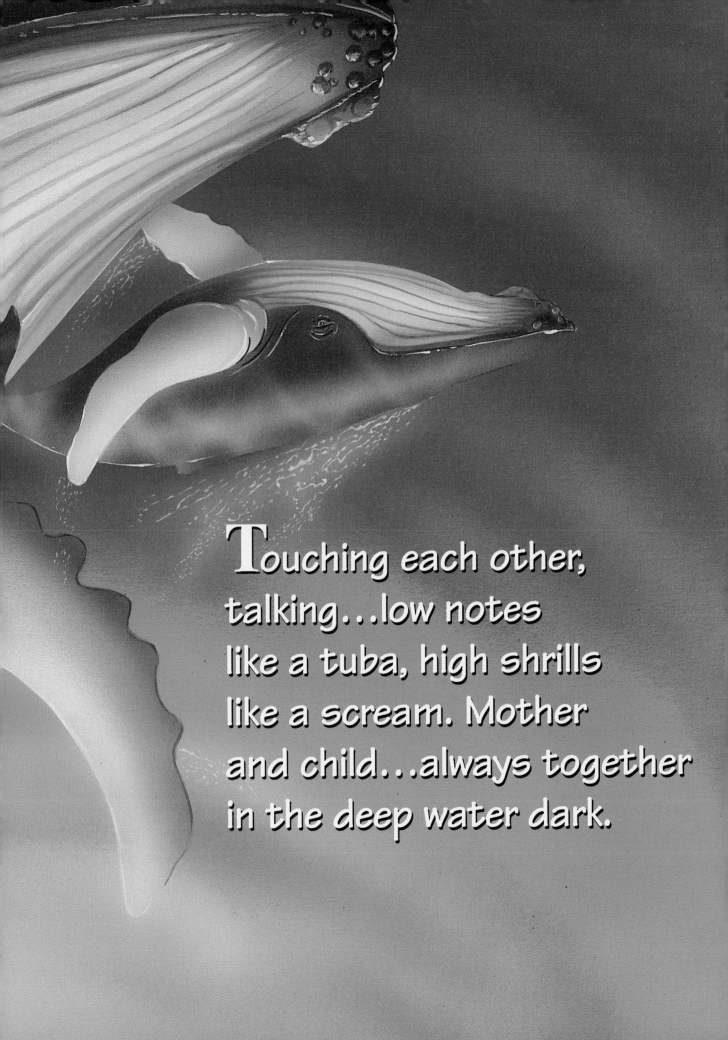

Touching each other,
talking...low notes
like a tuba, high shrills
like a scream. Mother
and child...always together
in the deep water dark.

The deep water dark,
the deep water dark,
singing, dancing
in the deep water dark.

A baby whale grows fast with 40 feedings a day. Swimming and drinking…all day long, surface and breathe…dive and drink.

The humpback whales,
with light blue above
and dark blue below…
hurtle skyward,
up, out of the water.
Limber gymnasts,
suspended in air,
then falling free…

These singing whales, gentle sea creatures, dive, diving deep, carry musical secrets through the deep water dark.